Mom -

I hope y

the author reaches English at Binghamton University (she became tenured eleven years ago at the age of 70).

Love,
Pete

SIMPLICITY

RUTH STONE

PARIS

PRESS

Northampton, Massachusetts

Library of Congress Cataloging-in-Publication Data
Stone, Ruth.
Simplicity / by Ruth Stone.
p.   cm.
ISBN 0-9638183-1-7
I.   Title.
PS3537.T6817S5   1995   94-40667

This book is a creative act. Any resemblance to persons living or
dead or to actual incidents or events is purely coincidental.

Paris Press books are published for Adrian Oktenberg in honor
of her mother, Roma Florence Paris, 1915-1992.

Paris Press, P.O. Box 267, Northampton, MA 01061-0267
2 3 4 5 6 7 8 9 0

For my poetry daughters

Ingrid Arnesen

Deborah Campbell

Jan Freeman

ACKNOWLEDGMENTS

Thanks to the following publications in which some of these poems first appeared: *The American Poetry Review*; *The American Voice*; *Boulevard*; *Choomia*; *Concourse 6*; *Footwork*; *New Myths/MSS*; *Poetry East*; *Shockbridge*; *Sojourner*; *Stardate*; *The Best American Poems of 1991*, edited by Mark Strand; *The Best American Poems of 1993*, edited by Louise Glück; *A Garden of Earthly Desserts*, edited by William Rossa Cole and Hilma Wolitzer; *WPFW 89.3 FM Poetry Anthology*, edited by Grace Cavalieri; *Nursery Rhymes From Mother Stone* (Mbira Press, Binghamton, NY, 1992); *The Solution* (Alembic Press, Ltd., Baltimore, MD, 1989).

Grateful acknowledgment is made to the Mrs. Giles Whiting Foundation for a Whiting Writers' Award which aided in the making of this book.

To Adrian, I feel honored to be a part of Paris Press. Working together has been a unique experience for me. This is what publishing should be. It has made me utterly happy.

Thanks to Ingrid, Deborah, and Jan, for sustenance.

CONTENTS

SIMPLICITY

LOOK TO THE FUTURE

To you born into violence,
the wars of the red ant are nothing;
you, in the heart of the eruption.

I am speaking from immeasurable grass blades.
You, there on the rubble,
what is the river of vapor to you?

You who are helpless as small birds
downed on the ice pack.
You who are spoiled as
commercial fruit by the medfly.

To you the machine guns.
To you the semen of fire,
the birth of the maggot in the corpse.

You, to whom we send these gifts;
at the heart of light we are crushed together.
When the sun dies we will become one.

AGAINST LOSS

That time at the Down Beat: Billie Holiday.
Oh, nothing is succulent and sweet anymore.
We drank so much.
This was before the war, when we
were renting rooms for the weekends;
and you watched me brush my hair,
tickling your long fingers down my back.
I sometimes hear the trombone and sax and drums,
the wobble of spinning glass above the Ladies' Room,
where she was up-ending a little toff
of medicine out of a bottle.
I mean, Billie Holiday spoke to me down there.
She said, "I've got a bad cough," like an
apology. And I remember her.
Memory becomes the exercise against loss.
Later, when we were naked on the bed,
and that tremble of heat lightning along the muscles,
you began the slow measures of "Dover Beach"
in the only voice — the only voice —
"Ah, love, let us be true to one another."

RIPPLE EFFECT

You don't want to hate this world.
The tassels of corn don't.
Even though they've been forced into slavery *um*.
they never think of their heads chopped off,
only of turning into starch.
Sugar into starch
is what they think.
And to think is to do.
Of course growing together has a ripple effect.
A field of corn repeats everything it hears.
"I ear what you say,"
says one stalk of corn to another.

PLUMBING

Plumbing is so intimate.
He hooks up your toilet.
He places a wax ring
under the vitreous seat
where your shit will go.
You are grateful to him.
He is a god with wrenches;
a quiet young man
using a flame torch.
He solders the joints.
He crawls through your dusty attic
over the boxes of doll furniture,
the trains, the ripped
sleeping bags, the Beatles posters,
the camp cots, the dishes, the bed springs,
to wire up the hot water tank.
And you admire him
as you would Saint Francis,
for his simple acceptance
of how things are.
And the water comes like a miracle.
Each time in the night
with your bladder full,
you rise from the bed.
And instead of the awful stench
of the day before and perhaps
even the day before that,
in a moment of pure joy
you smell nothing but the sweet
mold of an old house

and your own urine as it sloshes
down with the flush.
And you feel comfortable, taken care of,
like some rich Roman matron
who had just been loved by a boy.

IT FOLLOWS

If you had a lot of money
(by some coincidence
you're at the Nassau Inn in Princeton
getting a whiff of class)
and you just noticed two days ago
that your face has fallen,
but you don't believe it,
so every time you look in the glass
it's still hanging there where it wasn't.
Would you take the money you needed
for a new roof on your old house
(the house you're paying for
over and over in property taxes)
because it's been leaking for years
and you're tired of emptying buckets
and spraying for mold,
would you take that money
and get your face lifted?
Face-lift. They cut a slit
under your ears and pull up the slack
and they tack it with plastic.
Then they pull up the outer
skin and trim it because it's too long
and fasten that. (Your skin
pulls loose from the fat like chicken skin.)
Because once you were almost
as beautiful as Jane Wyman . . .
your friends all said that.
Of course at the time she was
married to Ronnie and you were

involved with the ASU —
a McCarthy suspect.
Forget about your neck.
They can't do that yet.
A face-lift lasts five years.
So you could go on being a member
of new-speak and re-entry —
with the unsung benefits
of radiation and by then
your roof would have rotted anyway.
Or been recycled by some corporate kid.
But think how you'd rather
be stripped and streaked
and while you're about it
get some implants of baby teeth buds
that they've taken from dead babies' gums
and frozen for this sort of thing.
You could still die young.

THAT WINTER

In Chicago, near the lake, on the North Shore
your shotgun apartment has a sun room
where you indulge in a cheap
chaise lounge —
and read *Of Human Bondage* —
There is a window in the living-room proper
cracked open so your
Persian cat can go outside.
You are on the first floor and upstairs
a loud-mouthed southern woman,
whose husband is away
all week on business trips,
has brought her maid
up from Georgia
to do the work and take care of the baby.
"O Lord," the southern woman says,
"he wants it spotless on the weekend —"
The maid, who has
smooth brown skin,
is not allowed to sit on the toilet
but she feeds the kid
and changes the dirty diapers.
She washes the dishes,
she cooks the southern meals,
she irons the sheets for the mahogany bed.
The southern woman shouts
at her in a southern drawl,
"Junie, don't sit on that chair
you'll bust it."
The southern woman is at

loose ends five days
waiting for him to come in.
"It's like a honeymoon,
honey," she says —
"When he grabs me,
whooee."
She invites you up and makes
sure you understand
the fine points of being a white woman.
"I can't let her live
here — not in Chicago.
I made her go out
and get herself a room.
She's seventeen.
She bellered and blubbered.
Now I don't know
what she's trackin' in
from men."
It is winter. The ice
stacks up around the
retaining wall —
the lake slaps over
the park benches,
blocks of ice green with algae.
You are getting your mail secretly at a postal box
because your lover is in the Aleutians.
It's during the war and
your disgusting husband
works at an oil refinery
on the South Side.
Up there in the Aleutians
they are knocking the gold
teeth out of the dead Japanese.

One construction worker
has a skin bag with fifty
gold-filled teeth.
He pours them out at
night in his Quonset hut.
He brags about bashing their faces in.
One day you are fooling
around in a downtown music store
waiting for the war to end.
You let a strange teenage boy
talk you into going
home with him.
He lives alone in a basement behind a
square of buildings.
He shows you his knife collection
and talks obsessively about Raskolnikov — suddenly
your genes want to live
and you pull away
and get out of there.
It is almost dusk.
You run until you find the boulevard
sluggish with the 1943 traffic.
You know by now there
isn't much to live for
except to spite Hitler —
The war is so lurid
that everything else is dull.

PUTTING IT OFF

The dye was always a sick yellow.
We dipped everything in it.
Was I shoveled in with the others?
No one answered me.
There were no mouths.
When I spoke to Tricky Dick
it was always in the privacy of my own home.
He and Adolph lay under my bed.
You dogs settle down, I would say.
I'll take you to the vats tomorrow.

FOR EIGHT WOMEN

Gender loyalty, alien to the pits and ducts of ourselves;
how to unscrew this pattern?

Now here's another matter: the season of bagworms;
and yet the moths were so random, so azure.

One lives alone out of circumstance until the face
in the multiple mirrors is sour dough, full of its own gas.

The ocean is near, swallowing everything — a little cup
of water moving along the galaxy.

In Morocco my child goes down to the beach toward evening.
She forgets her tormentor, the headmaster's wife.

The ocean takes her, the broth of itself flowing inside her.
She rests with her feet in the scallops of water.

I cannot consider Canna, Alice or Shōkō without Verlaine,
Bashō or Connie Smith.

What is this pattern in the light of bagworms? Nevertheless,
the mornings here are a sweet shock to the blood.

The light as it falls on the louvered windows,
a pattern of slits, and above that, the balconies.

For a short time you are a stranger. Then the vision fades.
Then you become the door, opening and closing.

In the mountains, on my way home from the village, I would
pass my sister's grave. Embalming fluid is pink like antifreeze.

How red she looked in the casket. Next year her grave site caved in.
She stood on her head in the box. The sexton dumped in more dirt.

Dirt, dirty, soil is so useful. We track it in. The white carpet grows
yellow. Down here in the South along highways and boulevards,
        crepe myrtle.

I am a stranger crossing the bone bridge to meet the other.
Our skulls shine like calligraphy in a longed-for language.

YOU MAY ASK

When I think of how we shared the bathroom,
the phone, the cutlery.
How Tom's ex-boyfriend called up and said
Tom could come home anytime.
He said it in a long significant undertone . . .
And Clyde, who had broken with Igor,
because Igor moved when his former girlfriend
came with her mother and a truck
and took away all the basic furniture.
And Clyde's other lover ripped
out the phone by its roots.
All this time I was sleeping on Clyde's
dirty mattress with borrowed sheets
and all over New York they were dying of it.
Every time I opened the door,
a complete rack of Clyde's suits in my only closet.
And then I had to meet Clyde in Soho
at the Cupping Place to get his key,
where I thought he looked awfully used up.
Because Gertrude had locked me out,
although I had let her have my bed while I was gone
because she was desperate
and had fought with her landlady
and threw a fit and cried in front of everyone
about the laboring classes even though
she works for five lawyers
and her folks are OK in Brooklyn
and she reads her resistance rap everywhere
with a lot of feeling and makeup,
even false eyelashes, I worry.
How catching is it?

RESONANCE

The universe is sad.
I heard it when Artur Rubenstein played the piano.
He was a little man with small hands.
We were bombing Germany by then.
I went to see him in a dark warehouse
where a piano had been placed for his practice —
or whatever he did before a recital.
He signed the book I had with me —
it was called *Warsaw Ghetto*.
I later heard about him —
his affairs with young women —
if only I had known — but I was
in love with you.
Artur is dead;
and you, my darling,
the imprint of your face, alert like a deer —
oh god, it is eaten away —
the earth has taken it back;
but I listen to Artur —
he springs out of the grave —
his genius wired to this tape —
a sad trick of the neural pathways resonating flesh
and my old body remembers the way you touched me.

THE WOUND

[handwritten: end-stopped stanzas.]

The shock comes slowly
as an afterthought.

First you hear the words
and they are like all other words,

ordinary, breathing out of lips,
moving toward you in a straight line.

Later they shatter
and rearrange themselves. They spell

something else hidden in the muscles
of the face, something the throat wanted to say.

Decoded, the message etches itself in acid
so every syllable becomes a sore.

The shock blooms into a carbuncle.
The body bends to accommodate it.

A special scarf has to be worn to conceal it.
It is now the size of a head.

The next time you look,
it has grown two eyes and a mouth.

It is difficult to know which to use.
Now you are seeing everything twice.

After a while it becomes an old friend.
It reminds you every day of how it came to be.

[handwritten left margin: Broken up]
[handwritten: Sibilance & despite the dissonant images of poem]

THE NEWS

What have you to say to that
contorted gunned-down pile of rags
in a road; possibly nameless
even to the one who throws it
on a cart and pushes it away.

The discarded *New York Times*
is wrapped around your garbage,
a now wet, on-the-scene still
from someone's news camera,
stained with scraps from your kitchen.

And whose illusion that woman running
with a child? Already struck,
the machine gun crossing the line
of her body yet she does not fall
although she is already dead —

her history written backward —
There is no time to weep
for her. This was once the snot of semen,
the dim blue globe of the egg
moving through the fallopian tube.
That single body casting itself into the future.

THAT DAY

Since then we've gone around the sun fifty times.
The sun itself has rushed on.
All the cells of my skin that you loved to touch
have flaked away and been renewed.
I am an epidermal stranger.
Even enormous factories. So much.
Even the railway station —
ball-wracked. Eliminated.
Now the dead may be pelletized,
disgorged as wafers in space.
Some may be sent to the sun in casks,
as if to Osiris.
Where is that day in Chicago
when we stood on a cement platform,
and I held your hand against my face,
waiting for a train in the warm light?
That given moment-by-moment light,
which, in a matter of hours from then,
had already traveled out of the solar system.

THINGS I SAY TO MYSELF WHILE HANGING LAUNDRY

If an ant, crossing on the clothesline
from apple tree to apple tree,
would think and think,
it probably could not dream up Albert Einstein.
Or even his sloppy mustache;
or the wrinkled skin bags under his eyes
that puffed out years later,
after he dreamed up that maddening relativity.
Even laundry is three dimensional.
The ants cross its great fibrous forests
from clothespin to clothespin
carrying the very heart of life in their sacs or mandibles,
the very heart of the universe in their formic acid molecules.
And how refreshing the linens are,
lying in the clean sheets at night,
when you seem to be the only one on the mountain,
and your body feels the smooth touch of the bed
like love against your skin;
and the heavy sac of yourself relaxes into its embrace.
When you turn out the light,
you are blind in the dark
as perhaps the ants are blind,
with the same abstract leap out of this limiting dimension.
So that the very curve of light,
as it is pulled in the dimple of space,
is relative to your own blind pathway across the abyss.
And there in the dark is Albert Einstein
with his clever formula that looks like little mandibles
digging tunnels into the earth
and bringing it up, grain by grain,

the crystals of sand exploding
into white hot radiant turbulence,
smiling at you, his shy bushy smile,
along an imaginary line from here to there.

THEOLOGY

I am writing a poem
on the back of a grocery list
while all the time
pale pulsing heads of lettuce
are being chopped off
in the irrigated fields;
as samurai,
leaping forward with a scream,
once chopped the heads
of lazy clip-clopping peasants.
Those long trusting rows of green knobs
upfolded as so many thin veined
holy hands blessing the nitrates,
the sulfides,
the throb of the crop duster.

NS AT LUNCH ON THE BUS

← mundane, normal, almost not worthy of attention.

First they unzip the dark suitcase. [1]
The more sedate one pulls out the plastic bag. [2]
The other one zips the reticule and stretches
to put it up on the rack. With a smile she looks around. [3]
It is a small congratulation. [4]
Then they sit together. [5]
A paper napkin is spread on each ample lap. [6]
There is a momentary pause, almost breathless, [7] ← anticipation.
and then their delicate flesh fingers hold the sandwiches. [8]
As they bite, they brush away the crumbs. [9]
Their jaws, sensuous and steady, masticate the ham and cheese. [10]
They wear draped heavy head covers, [11]
dark coats and sensible dark oxford shoes. [12]
Under their habits: beige skin, the beige of their plump bodies, [13]
matrons who have given themselves. [14]
Under their dark belts, below the layers of man-made fibers; [15]
under their modest belly buttons, [16]
the unscarred skins of their stomachs; [17]
their organs, finally satiated, begin spasms of kneading, [18]
softening the mass with pepsins and acids, [19]
shoving it down into the bowels. [20]
Now they pour coffee into Styrofoam
and lift it to their lips. [21]
Then, mother of us all! [22]
some little chocolate cakes come peeping forth
and are tucked into their benevolent mouths
with a gentle sucking and swallowing. [23]
And then they tidy up. [24]
The thermos top is screwed on. The lint brushed. [25]

Has turned the mundane into a sensuous event

Clean up.

Paper napkins touched to their faces, their fingers. [26]
The plastic pouch is stowed away. [27]
And they settle to their deeper contemplations: [28]
the body of truth, the temporal body, the vessel of love. [29]

29/33 Lines

enstopped.

ROCKS RISING

Leone and Charles have painted their names
on big red rocks in Arizona.
Also Gerty and Dave, Toots and Tad
and the scouts from Troop Eleven.
"Hello" is spelled on the outcropping.
Head after head of rock is pushed up,
not even the brain of a chicken among them.
"Hi there." They slump among themselves.
The rocks peek over the dun-colored slope.
It's taken them a long time but they don't care.
"Yea for T.H.S.," they shout.
"Fuck the scout master."

THE USUAL

On the morning of the reading,
the room looks raw. You are not quite
yourself after the flu. Your poems
seem out-of-date. In two weeks
the world of outraged statement
has moved into a high-tech bomb area.
The newscasts are pure poetry.
Your sickness still sweats out of you.
What is significant; their fathers hunt
with machine guns, automatic rifles,
everything is known at the molecular level,
the possibilities of sex have gone into
the twenty-first century. Finally all
the poor die and we are left with only
the sick. Now we are all caring. Caring
is incorporated; it rallies on the stock
market. Caring is up two points. Euthanasia
is even with pork bellies. Caring is now done
by a discreet squad. They have gone back
to the swastika. Because of the fumes they
have all shaved their heads. The sick are
again marked with tattooed blue numbers.
You decide when they come they will find you have
hung yourself in the closet. They will fumigate.

enjambment.

Still simple

change
her
line breaks.
Still uses
Simple
sentences.

THE WOMAN IN THE TV

The dark TV screen reflects the lamp;
the lamp and the windows.
And through the windows,
sunlight on the house next door.

In the dim room
inside the dark TV screen,
I see that a woman lives in there.
Sometimes she lies in bed all day.

Sometimes she thinks about the dark mountains;
the sharp outcroppings
that bristle with stunted pines,
the bare rock patches like diseased skin,
the trees like unwanted facial hairs.

She knows that the mountains can be seen
even at night; black against black.

The woman in there is heavy
like the raw-faced rocks;
the rocks that are bare even of snow,
when snow lies like a sickness,
like peeling skin on the pits and scars
of the thin soil in the crevices.

Sometimes the woman in the dark TV
pulls me to her.
"Draw the blinds," she whispers,
"and turn on the set —
so I can get out —
so we can be together."

METAMORPHOSIS

One day you wake up and you have a new face.
What's this? you say
in the harsh kosher manner
of your mother-in-law in a high-class restaurant.

Although your hair is Titian red
and not blue rinse like hers,
she always sent whatever it was back —
No matter how many times you look in the mirror
you can't make it go away.

So this is it.
All those women
you thanked God you didn't look like
have surfaced from caves in your cells
where they have been waiting for years
to gather you into their coven.

And now you remember her bitterness;
too much salt, burned edges;
it was never good enough.

THE QUESTION

While needles of the evergreen
practice a windy chaos,
heads of snarled hair;
something in the tree
longs for old age;
bald brown knobs of skull
without subterfuge;
but it continues with its greedy
resinous sexual odors.
The odors rise against one another,
spurting away from the scaly bark.
Along its fingers the tree
holds out microscopic traps.
Popping bullets of sunlight
crack into the subliminal
orifices, and the tree thinks,
"How exquisite. Is this love?"

POSSIBLY

I was taking a walk this morning with Bob.
He's the second man to nudge me and say,
"See that woman on the corner?
She's a prostitute."
"Well," I said, "I guess she is wearing leather
short shorts and a fur piece on a hot day
and purple glitter calf-high boots
and carrying a whip. But I thought
she was just waiting for the bus."
"Listen," Bob says, "I've been pushing Vera.
I want her to do well."
He was talking about Vera, his wife,
who is running against the current County Clerk.
"The corruption is so deep-seated in Lamoge County,
I mean, you can't sit for the shit," Bob says,
"but now there's never anyone at home
and I can't get on the phone. It's tied up.
It's getting so they call me Mr. Vera."
"I know," I say, "it's the same way with me.
You should have kept a sheet thrown over her."
And four days later he's got body lice.
He says he caught them from a dog.
"Oh, Bob," Vera says. "Why don't you
get out and make something of yourself?
Run for dog catcher, for God's sake!
You've got charisma."

MEDIUM FOR STASIS

She is in the center of the picture,
here on the bed, waiting for daylight.
If it is a gouache, or oil on paper,
the weight of her hips on the futon
will affect the brush strokes.
Some reflection from a round section
of clear glass slipped behind
the open bookcase, or the long
beveled mirror, could repeat certain parts
of her; an arm, even a finger if she
holds it out. The once cautious
transom, a form of inadequate escape
or peephole, has been irrevocably
painted shut. The books in the case
are all, one hundred of them,
about chess.

There is a Russian
chess player in the other room.
The canvas, or, if it is a watercolor,
the textured paper, will absorb
blue-green shadows. Her pink blouse
and front-fastened bra hang over
the chair facing the typewriter
which sits without changing expression
like a set of false teeth.
The art must include a tone,
a presence of the chess player.
Igor brought him in like a wet cat.
His charisma is poverty and mental preoccupation.
He plays the game for money.

Igor owes him money.
Watercolor would do as a medium,
even a fauve technique, a quick catch.

In here, her room, which is the first
of the triptychs, Igor has one shelf
of the bookcase filled with his shoes and perhaps
a pair of his old girlfriend's shoes.
They are all, like a drawer in the morgue,
possible clues; getting a little stiff,
without body heat or oil, the shine
of one metal buckle making a far-off moon.
Among them the old walking patterns;
worn spots on the soles characteristic
of the swing of the pelvis, the long
leg bones, the joints of the thigh;
those large sculptured hollows smooth
as wet clay, significant as any reamed out
by Henry Moore. This moment perhaps,
after all — collage.

            The flume of the building
is a center around a square hole of air.
Her window opens upon it; light comes down
as into a mine, a brick shaft.
It is a subdued filtering, too deep
for birds to explore.
At the bottom, trash cans, rubble,
where some of the bricks and mortar
from higher up have come down.

In a painting where bodies overlap
on the one dimensional surface,
the other side of the face, in a profile

for instance, is hidden; as the lower
half of a body in a casket is often
not dressed and seldom wears shoes.

The section of Yasha, asleep in the other
room where the fire escape is locked
with a steel grill across the window,
since getting in is more fearsome than
getting out; Yasha is lying on the bed
as he did when he was a child,
before his father was killed at the front
in World War II. Before his mother died
without recognizing his photograph
which he had sent to her in Moscow
from Israel where he had emigrated
and was in the army.
The effect is murky, an underground treatment,
the suggestion of buried lives.
One thinks of Lenin, dead of syphilis.

Igor, after creating this mirage,
puts on his long black coat
and goes out to be with his new
girlfriend who is editing film.
Igor is writing a film on the subject
of stasis. Nothing happening.
It is seven thirty-one in the morning.
The medium is everything.

It would be amusing to show Yasha
in the manner of Bonnard. Yasha is
slightly built, rather to become
in old age, stocky; but now frail,

a wide jaw and mild porpoise smile
with some obvious dental work;
the painting done with
that carelessly careful stroke
of the wrist, the brush; his slightly
moldy or slept-in brown suit, instantly
un-American. He is far from Russia,
from Israel, hanging out at the chess club
nearby and carrying pictures of himself
and other men hunched over chess boards,
all of male history built into their
tactical maneuvers. As Yasha says,
"Chess is like," many waves of his arms,
more and more teeth showing, "life,"
he says, pounding the back of one hand
into the palm of the other.

Perhaps Yasha is short because
Igor is tall. Igor is more
plastic, with pale skin and straw-colored hair,
tall and skinny; a retired jock,
an athlete gone bad, who proofreads for the
Wall Street Journal and something else and writes
metered inner-rhymed poetry and sublets and sub-sublets
this apartment. Meanwhile, all the furniture
is gradually going out the front door;
today, the old Persian rug.

Yasha's father was killed at the front
in winter. Not by the SS. No, he was
a foot soldier, a replacement
in the endless conscription.
For thirty-eight years Yasha and his mother

stayed on in Moscow; electrical engineering,
the certificate. But with him
it was always the game for money.
However, the Russians don't really
want the Russian Jews to win.
It was difficult. He emigrated to Tel Aviv.
In order to stay he had to serve
in the Israeli army.

In the lesser painting
(possibly only a photograph), the kitchen;
she is in a corner chair by the small
green desk where cautious cockroaches
inspect her before advancing to the stove.
She is having coffee in this spot for the last
time as the desk is also going out to the old
girlfriend's today. The chairs, Igor tells her,
will remain. The wiring in the overhead lights
is gone. Evidence of small fires among
the twisted fixtures. Yasha is still behind
the closed door.

Immediately after Igor leaves,
Yasha becomes confiding. A pan of water is heating
in the kitchen. Steam requires delicate handling,
especially against tan walls. Watercolor, or
Cray-pas. Perhaps a mixture with ink lines.
He tells her about his mother refusing to
move away from Moscow. How he lost an
important chess game because of her death.
Everyone took up a collection so he
could go visit her at the hospital.
"Not recognize me," he says with gestures.

He looks at her, sagging his lips.
Alone with a woman his manner becomes expectant.
They have tea. Not light enough for pointillism.
Perhaps a lithograph, or again, in the manner
of family portraits, a studio camera of the turn
of the century. The picture slightly going brown.

Here she is on the dirty foam rubber Hide-A-Bed couch
with her cup about to reach her lips, looking at
Yasha who is breaking a piece of sour cream cake
with his small fingers. The coffee table
will go soon, as Igor wants it in his new
girlfriend's apartment which can use
some more furniture.

          Igor, she sees in the future,
as balding; a little filled out the way athletes will.
As he moves from one spatial area to the next,
he leaves behind a litter of bodies in various
stages of frustration and orgasm.
These could also be part of the composition;
perhaps as small figures painted on china,
displayed here and there among the chess books.

The problems of being in the painting concern
angles of vision. As from the bedroom window,
she sees the lamp in the living room window,
its twin on her table in this room.
Her shoes, too, are in the painting;
flat and black, with straps,
like the child's shoes in a Mary Cassatt.
Her feet are in them hanging over the edge
of the bed. The flesh tones are mottled. A work of art

is a possible stasis where nothing is happening.
Where the energy of what has happened
stops at the moment of what will happen.

THE SPERM AND THE EGG

The sperm hate the egg.
They are afraid of it.
An ogress.
They clot the hot
red anteroom,
clinging to the walls.
She is blue and pulsing.
They are small and inadequate
and lose their tails.
Their chlorine milk begins to spoil.
But on the journey
when the shudder swept them
into an excited knot and
expelled them all together,
early sight scattered ahead of them.
They traveled like a shower of comets.
It was as if they were the universe.

The egg puts out her slimy pseudopod
and takes the sperm into the jelly.
The sperm is hysterical.
Now the egg is busy changing shape.
The sperm does not want to
be pulled apart into strings.
"Don't unravel me," it cries.
The egg does not hear it.
Deep inside the sperm
a seething hatred for the egg.
"When I had my tail,

I was free," the sperm cries.
It remembers the ultimate
vast trajectory.
It remembers them all crying,
"To be or not to be!"

My talk to you, a continuous invention,
like a sailor's tatting;
the casual thread between fingers
becoming medallions.
Far back in the sailor's nebula of neurons,
the delicate spread of lace.

Hooking this word to this word,
my talk with you is a slip-stitch,
a French-knot;
embroidery over the plain cloth
of waking and sleeping.

Upstairs in the back room,
my unfinished appliqué quilt,
folded away year after year,
with the same last stitch
and the same motionless needle.

My talk with you is not like the red-wing
or nuthatch,
not so practical now.
More like the snowmelt
that cannot be stopped.
Cold and liquid,
its crystals shattered,
its pendulous breasts and testicles
rotting together;
the sweat of the snow

without muscle or will,
the plaything of gravity
says what I say to you:
the babble of nothing to nothing.

A COMPARISON

Water —
the crystal mirage;
as in this suburb
where snow falls every day,
even in sunlight;
veils, transformed images
feathered white;
gloved bracts and pods —
irrefutable marriages.

Love also takes its shape
from climate,
performing miracles of art;
is also ninety per cent of the body,
which cannot live without it;
is used again and again,
the workhorse of the world;
and yet, so delicate.

ISOLATION

It is a good thing to look down
into the apartment across the courtyard;
to see a woman in there, her silhouette
wavering as a fish in shallows.
Or to vibrate in the full hum of the two
door refrigerator recovering slowed-down
molecules from expanded coolants.

Under the new Victorian lamp,
the left hemisphere, anxious as a fist,
waits for heavy steps across the cable.
Outside, inside, every hair phosphorescent —
dangerous pits, the violent flaking surfaces
of the hands, the feet,
like a steady rain of plankton.

The woman across the courtyard has
turned out the light. She has
gone deep, giving up oxygen,
into the lower levels of concrete.
Between us, the bloom of uncompacted garbage
throws a net of spores swarming around her,
a fine putrid gauze.
Now the umbilical cord between us snaps,
sparkling in the gray valley of Eighty-second Street.

Here, in the living room, I discover a briefcase.
Someone has forgotten it.
It is the transformed hide of a calf,
tortured from birth,

butchered on a moving belt,
skinned by automatic hands.
It is leaning, clear as an oil painting,
against the wall.
Our pulses coordinate.
A message is coming. It is crossing
vast distances, photon by photon.

VICTORIAN LAMP ON MY DESK

From the lead angels strapped by the groins
to opposite sides of the lead column, you can only deduce
their desire to rise; their outstretched arms,
only the toes of their right feet touching the base,
their left legs stepping out into space.
But it is in their mouths,
open to drink the clouds they cannot reach,
and how their upper teeth show in a latent animal
despair, that they are frozen in the hell of artifice.

DÉJÀ VU

Is it that every rainy day
will bring back the same feeling?
Glistening asphalt running like a deep river
through my dreams. Drowned telephone poles,
traffic lights; the softly thundered shower.
Seven o'clock. An empty parking lot
passive as the hide of a sleeping amoeba.
Other than this gray common denominator,
your breathless silence. Lost outline
of fields where streets ended in flowers;
lines that crossed once; the metaphysics of sorrow.
So slight, and yet the same pulsing
arteries of trees. Your shadow
intersecting without dimension.
I walk always in the direction of nothing;
the rain coming in gusts,
shaking me as water from the leaves.   *Sibilance.*

THE GAME

Saturday in Binghamton, love,
east of the Alleghenies, darling,
in footwear city;
you wouldn't believe it!
I sit here in outlet boots
and navy Air Force pants. Friend,
it snows.
I'm off duty.
During the week I wear
my writer-in-residence clothes;
the same black skirt,
an interchangeable top,
iron-maiden bra with steel stays,
Italian pumps from Ames
and panty hose.
We know the game's perverse.
But not so perverse
as when I drew with death
for your kiss and got the short end.

Stoma; that's a black hole.
The photon falls (he doesn't
catch on) into the maelstrom.
Ping, ping, down the staircase.
"Oh, sugar!" he says in exasperation.
He kicks the sweet thing waiting in the dark.
FLASH! It's all over.
The $C_{12}H_{22}O_{11}$ shrugs and becomes starch.
Already the battered $C_6H_{10}O_5$
has had enough of his passion.
The ambition of $C_{55}H_{72}O_5N_4M_g$ seizes her.
"Give me air," she shouts, "give me air and water!
I'm going to the top.
I'm going to make that green stuff."

PROPHETS

A dead steer bloating by the fence
is a broadside sermon:
O Lord, I am not as the others —
turning grass into the two-legged.

And the tenderness of trash pits
along the roadsides of towns
cry out: *Give us the bodies of your old cars*
and we can grow deep as Nineveh.

What is that bird saying?
He is not just saying, "Here I am
and my nephews may not approach."
The entourages of plumage
in the courtly oak
are all another species.
"And you, my consort, my basket,
my broody decibels,
my lover in the lesser scales;
this is our tree, our vista,
our bagworms.
In short, tra la,
my territory.
Ah, but the sky straight up
is also mine.
This is the clear advantage
of my wings.
Also the sun;
my morning orange to you, my dear . . .
and so on."
This is what he sings.

ABOUT RABBITS

Baby rabbits kick up their legs.
What cunning mouthfuls.
Is it play?
Yes. It is the leap against gravity.
Ask me another.
Is it the object which
excites the photons?

Put it this way.
Here is a bed.
Lie down and close your eyes.
The universe is an enormous hydrocephalic brain.
We and the rabbits are in this giant head.
In other words,
we see what we see.

Under the hard moon
the rabbits leave
small tracks
in the snow.
Protons, neutrons, charms,
gamma rays, neutrinos.

WE ARE ALL PARTICLES
OF THIS

Uncle Anti
on my mother's side,
died of inflamed desertion
in the Spanish American War.
He swelled at the joints.
He was not the bride of the cavalry.
He was a sick honcho.
Teddy Roosevelt did not care
that Uncle Anti's temperature
was a hundred and three.
"We must free these little
bastards," he said.
Dishonorable discharge to the head.
My Uncle Anti
came home broken,
and died in Grandma's feather bed.
Family myth. The universe bled;
a positive sign.
Teddy made his mark:
quark! quark!
All this time the infrared
knew something . . .
"The weak is a force you have
not reckoned with."

FEATHERS

Someone on a small red snow blower —
it's my neighbor who makes porch furniture,
or his daughter who takes vials of blood and urine
in racks on a tinkling cart for analysis,
or helps hook up the dialysis patient.
The hospital is just two blocks. You hear the sirens.
One of my neighbors goes along the walk and makes a path.
In five minutes it's covered up. It's bracing
to jog through. Mounded like Grandma's beds,
the puffs shaken and filled with air. A molecular down.
My mother said you weren't allowed to sit on the bed
when she was young. Her mother was house-proud.
When I knew Grandma she was strong but shrunken,
and raising Aunt Mabel's wild boys. She kept
a wood-burning cast-iron stove going and polished it
with cooking grease; but her teeth were gone.
Grandma always had a springhouse back then, where the water
flowed through to keep the butter she churned
from going bad. The water was so cold and clear, she said.
A steady downfall, no gusts or flurries. They've given up
on the blower. Their black cat, watching from across the street,
suddenly runs, belly close to the ground, toward the privet hedge.
Under the mysterious transformed water, the mysterious
earth, out there moving among the stars all by itself,
moving along a path, turning and singing,
with this life that it carries.

THE UNGRATEFUL

When you deprive yourself, I said to my body,
whose face gets wrinkled? Yours or mine?
She was suffering apathy.
We sat on the porch, a glass of wine between us,
honeysuckle blotting up the sky.
Many objects are strewn
in the fashion of insane old women who
have blocked the doorways with chiffoniers.
In case of fire they will burn with their obsessions.
Trees have seeded themselves in all the flower beds,
a willful violence between the arteries;
entire barns of debris, boxes from flea markets,
nails, empty oil cans, broken hoses.
The strangle underground rages in white rooted pulp.
I am leaving you, says my body;
her black moles, eyes of skin,
looking in all directions.
She, for whom I sacrificed everything,
with whom I shared every indignity.

ROTTEN SAMPLE

I travel like a salesman with my samples.
A little of this and that,
a ghostly other-than, including a dead whale
brought in a boxcar to Indianapolis.
We stood in line. My boyfriend (this was in the Thirties)
killed everything but people at that time.
Last night the whale's putrid odor returned.
I do not dream. I travel with a ream of bond.
I am a Gemini. My doppelgänger
sometimes speaks for me.
Oi, have you got blubber, she says.

SPLIT, CONJUGATE, WHATEVER

The plastic cup is empty.
All of the frozen chocolate has been eaten.
The forest of the tongue giving succor
to the desires of its strange animals.
Tiny pronged heads of skin-tissue flowers
quiver with textural pleasure.
In the homely cave of the mouth,
ancient indigenous populations
begin to have sex and multiply.

NURSERY RHYME

The hair of the planet grows thin,
glaciers have pocked its skin.
The hole above its head
like a leaking artery,
pumps out the magnetic flow
from its iron and nickel heart.
Armless, legless, an egg,
it drags a deep weight of ice,
and we are its fleas, its lice.

Does she love this monster in blue,
this spoiling water-wrapped kid?
She gongs and sings and throbs.
It hangs in her plasma womb
with its blemishes and blights,
a little seed gone bad,
her only viable spawn,
this sickening pippin dwarf
ravaged with parasites.

AS MIRACLES GO

While I was gone
the invisible alchemist
who lives in my house when I'm away
was still trying to make gold
out of nail clippings,
baking soda and llama fuzz.
What a fool!
This time I return to a carafe of five
gelatinous purple-skinned mice,
drowned and bloated in the leftover coffee,
the plastic lid snapped down on the carafe.
They float in a circle as if they are
chasing each other nose to tail.
How long they have looked with insane hope,
their pink eyes staring out of this glass wall
at the wavering kitchen;
the pale spread pads of their feet
suppliant as the hands of novitiates.

A VERY STRETCHED SENNETT

Some things like the fat policeman and the black prostitute
aren't fit for sonnets. But the form for today
is fourteen lines iambic pentameter. Won't compute.
Maybe by cheating a little I can get away
with passing this off. Think of a Mack Sennett
comedy in black and white, say Oliver Hardy
is the cop. He's dragging this would-be tenant
of the bus station, a skinny black party
girl. She's screaming, dress up to her crotch. His arms
are holding her. It's very sexual.
They go the length of the station. Her charms
are obvious. He loves it. He's got her flesh. We all
want to applaud. Finally he throws her out the door. We yawn.
Now he's center front, rubbing his hands, smiling. Then she's
    back inside and he's chasing her again and so on.

FLASH

1.

The poetry factory is canning W.W. type
good gray poems this week.
The help are wearing fake gray beards.
Everything has flannel backing.
An especially drab straw boss
comes over the intercom.
Watch it, he says. No funny business.
This grass isn't what you think it is.

2.

A bulletin from the poetry factory says —
we like our images stuck on with mortician's wax.
Mix 'em, don't match 'em.
Another dense article
on the craft of extracting.
Any size, shape, content.
Test a few.
Our G.N.P. is poetry.
Catalog on request.
All poems are pressed.
May our salesmen call on you?

3.

There is an austerity drive
on at the poetry factory.
Only one, two words to a line.
Thinner, the boss shouts.
Get those poems long and skinny.
Stretch that content.
Get those empties rolling.
Show me the whites of them pages.

ORDER AND DESIGN

Compare the galaxy to a night of fireworks;
exploding phosphenes, mirror images.
Shine the house, rearrange furniture.
You are tracing mandalas lit inside the skull.
The calm and ordinary
is always based on a most delicate rite.
This chair placed on the unseen loop
of a circle, the housekeeper in the continuum
coming from deep within the brain
and departing at the speed of light.

ON THE WAY

He is standing at the window of the train
as if facing the sacred,
his lips mouthing a prayer.
Metal storage sheds and clustered low-cost housing
string along the tracks;
a June flush of leaves and wild mustard.
After the prayer, he sticks out his tongue
like a snake flicking for heat,
and opens his mouth, showing his teeth
as if cleansing, and swallows.
He is well dressed in a western-style suit,
but his wife wears a sari, sandals and
a small jeweled gold ring in one nostril.
The plowed Ohio fields, already dust-dry,
windbreaks along the fences,
osage orange and ailanthus, tree of heaven.
The young man looks at what we cannot see.
The train rocks toward Chicago.
There, in a Jewish graveyard, you lie
between your mother and your father.
Your father, the devout cantor,
and your mother, the Orthodox housekeeper.
While I, the Aryan skeptic,
loose flesh on the bones of an old woman,
am carried as if on the back of an ass.
I, the gift of my father,
the original bride arriving,
already shorn for the wedding,
at the gates of your city.

RITUAL

Two girls outside the train
are talking about their clothes.
One is fingering and explaining
her hand-knit sweater.
Facing away from the wind,
she lights a cigarette.
The other, with her back to us,
raises and drops her arms
like a wooden clack toy;
and then, so serious,
they look at each other.
The one puts her hand on her hip,
and the other drops her cigarette
and steps on it.
We know the stickiness of parting,
ritual repeated words,
the dark divided brain with its eyes
on the cold passage.

OTHERWISE

Under other conditions, the dinner napkin
hanging over the back of the wicker chair
could be the surface of the moon.
We understand it is the moon,
our collective satellite.
And the child — whose head
could have been painted by Raphael —
is slowly plunging into space
from the foam mattress;
his red hair leaping out, electric
as the visions under his fused skull.
As well as the older dog,
who has taken the lower section
of the mattress, and is curled,
also compartmentalized in space,
even farther than the moon.
And this, under other conditions,
could be heaven or hell or limbo.
And we understand that it is our
collective desire to understand.

OTHER

Why am I not that brown-skinned man
who passes my train window?
His face looks disappointed,
his lips scornful, their shape
translated in terms of my life;
my own life — that dark
slippery strip of film.
Now we are moving apart —
the silver body of the train
pushing against the air,
parting the streams of gasses.
Where is he now?
His face looks back at me
out of my face reflected in the window.
I feel his clothes;
his stomach muscles contracting,
his own familiar legs, like mine,
not firm as they once were,
sometimes cramping at night
even in his sleep,
his feet, calloused along one side,
a little fungus between the toes.
Yet, his legs are taking him somewhere.
I will never know who puts their arms
around him, if they do,
or who hands him his junk mail
in a men's only hotel.
In the capsule of the train
the shaded wings of his body
press against me;
I taste the wafer of my bitterness.

And then, the soft umber of snow change,
the land turning faster,
heads of tall grasses gone to seed,
pools of melted snow beside the tracks.

AS I REMEMBER

She was his secretary, he was head
of the Ku Klux Klan in Indiana.
She was twenty years old when they found her dead

body. It was suicide. She was in his bed
room at French Lick, where the Klan ran a
weekend body politic. She was his efficient secretary, he was head.

She grew up in Irvington. Rape, the newspapers said.
She cut her throat. Let us say her name was Anna.
She was just twenty years old when they found her dead.

This was in the Twenties, before bread,
even at four cents a loaf, became a luxury. Yes, this was when the
    stock market sang hosanna.
When she graduated from business school in downtown
    Indianapolis, and rose to be his secretary, her family was
    proud, he was the Grand Wizard, he was head.

She was a lovely average weight and height, her Presbyterian
    character, thread by thread,
fine as damask for an altar cloth. She worked assiduously for him.
    Her skin would have been like Lana
Turner's, blonde; she had not even cut her blonde hair when they
    found her dead.

The Klan's white-pillared antebellum headquarters in Irvington,
    spread
across the *Indianapolis Star*. It was a big banana.
She was his private secretary. A front page head.

And anyway, the State's Attorney and the Governor's opponents were fed
up with the Klan's bloody hands in their tills. Their plan: a
state-wide campaign to clean up scandal; when they fortuitously found her dead.

He served part of his prison term (in luxury). The Democrats got in office, led
by the Citizens for Decency. When the manna
of heaven falls where she bled, if it falls, let it spring up in Venus
flytraps stinking of rotten meat. He was the Klan's Grand Mogul. He was head.

"Poor girl," my grandmother would say,
"if she'd carried red pepper in her handkerchief,
or gone to college, she'd be here today."

THE SYSTEM

As shade preserves for a moment,
the dead mole — her purple velour coat,
the quiet dignity of her tough snout,
beetles carry her away
in decent discreet packages. In a slight measure,
make it possible for us to breathe
and walk every day over that pile,
as she liquefies to carrion.
And flies, good creatures that they are,
deposit a swarm of maggots in her,
to work in thrifty progression;
the fire of her particles
splitting their pale fat skins
growing along the lattice
with bristly hairs,
thousands of lenses,
suction cups of intractable feet,
as they labor in the bondage of form.

GETTING THERE

The Blue Ridge fades behind a row
of buck-toothed trailers. Driving the slack
valley on slattern two-lane roads
you're forced to the shoulders, chickened on the curves
by head-on brand new pickups coming down the middle.
Yes, ma'am! Hibiscus blooming wild along
their nasty barbed wire fence, and you
stop in a grocery –filling station to
make change. They don't allow no checks.
A plastic stack of white bread on the tacky counter
and a bilious assortment of rifle cartridges.
Depends on how you look at it. How?
They're staring at you. A punk swell of restless boys
pooling a six-pack. You put money in the phone
and listen with your back turned. There's no answer.
You put your money in your purse. The woman
behind the counter drawls, "Y'all come back now."

HOW IT CAME TO BE

Once
a bear who couldn't sleep through the winter
fished the full moon out of a lake
and hung it in her cave.
"There," she said, "in essence,
can there be another like me?"
Echo came back, "Incandescence."
"That's it, bulb," she cried,
"You turn me on!"
And she went right out and got lit.
Edison obtained wind of this
and stole the whole thing,
and that's why it isn't dark any more.

The plastic is waiting in rolls.
It can never be full enough.
Everything is seen through it.
Among the dry goods, the smell of indelible ink
enters everyone's brain.
Blouses, coats, panties breathing together.
The air in the Variety Store comes up from the basement
where the shoes, as in a cryptorium, one box above the other,
lie in their cardboard nests.
Customers coming in,
the pearl buttons sewn to paper packets
prepare to be chosen.
Their voices become a little sharp.
It is the same with them every day.
They have grown old together without knowing it.
The ladies behind the counters take great scissors
and cut through bolts of material with unusual zest.
It is the first or the last morning of the final summer.
The hardware department coils in snakes of garden hoses,
and indispensable rubber washers wink at themselves.

LEAVING NEW YORK WITH HARRY

He's in another seat of the bus
taking a nap. And he won't do.
Your silent dialogue with me
and mine with you, our blank page,
foolscap on which we write nothing,
lies between us. I look out the window.
Gulls, white as new cut limestone,
tilt in sculptured pairs
over the soft broom of last year's rushes.
You ripple through me like slant light
on the New Jersey meadows.

What are we now, old remnant, worn filament?
Only an imprint of the naked bulb
that burned all night above our bed,
that seared our existential madness,
as if we had been stitched together
by a surgeon at all our openings —
as if we lay inside one another
as in a Klein bottle,
the stamp of extermination on our foreheads.

A LOVE LIKE OURS

Once upon an avenue a small crack
smiled at a linden tree.
"I love your dappled shadow," it thought;
but only to itself.
The small crack stretched with pleasure.
The pure meld of the sun boiled
at its fragmented edges.
"How I crumble," the crack whispered,
"how the weight and the shock go through me.
I am a true MacAdam."
The linden tree shook itself in the jet stream.
It hummed with wings.
Male and female, pollen and pistil; it hummed.
Toward the equinox the air was filled with
a riding of seeds. They went in pushing crowds,
kicking and falling. They prickled the street
with their adolescent bursting.
In the morning the street cleaner,
gushing water, rolled over them
with thousands of bristles.
It brushed them along in a stream to the gutter.
One shy young linden seed was swept into the crack.
The crack gave a sigh.
At last it knew that the linden tree had noticed.
"A love like ours," said the crack,
"could split the street, could break up traffic!
Given time, it could even damage the sewer!"

LIVING SPACE

Up here, the folks who live in trailers
are often large fat folks but sometimes
they are wizened older men living alone.
The trailer is often close to the road
and often when the snow melts, a confusion
of cast-off tires, a sagging woodshed
and the brilliance of plastic that floated
from passing hot rods during the long
winter afflicts a naked sadness. Inside
the trailer, it will be over-warm with
wall-to-wall red carpeting. The kitchen
end, snug, with a maple table and chairs,
Electro-Perk and a tree of coffee mugs.

With certain trailers, toward evening
several men will be standing near the road.
A car has stopped and the ones in the car
lean out and those on the bare ground
in front of the trailer (the spot that will
later bloom with orange daylilies) will
seem to be settling some intricate problem
in motors. There will be another car and
a truck. The hood of a blowzy Plymouth
will be up. Regular traffic slows down to get
past and the people driving by, if they look,
can see hairy arms and thick fingers upending
cans of beer. The skinny owner of one of the
cars will be leaning back against the trailer
dragging on a cigarette and shouting "Hey, Bucky"
to a Buick that screeches to a stop and then guns on.

Or a trailer can be fronted with a small porch
with iron railings and pots of geraniums and
fluffy white curtains at the windows.
Its owners are almost never visible though
often it, too, is close to the road.
The trailers with children running in
and out usually have a beaten defeated
patch of grass and almost always a dog
tied up without any water or food in its
plastic dog bowls. For those on a low
fixed income, trailers are almost as
affordable as small houses used to be.

If they catch fire they are apt to burn
at white heat. Like other people, the
people who live in trailers may have
rectangular minds, modules for large
color TV's. The bottom-heavy young wives
may shop in the evening at Ames, their
small children playing hide-and-seek in
the racks of nylon pantsuits. They live
in another space. They have settled close
to the earth. They have retained their
rugged American rights to their own home.

Often elderly couples have traded a trailer
for a camper and drive south in cold weather,
their whimsical vehicles wagging down the
crowded lanes, while up front, their stiff
silver-haired profiles are pointed like
migrating lemmings toward that which is
always out there in the great American dark.

TRASH

You want to forget it
like you want to forget
those women of no particular age
living on the sidewalks;
bloated trash bags,
display of matted heads
pulled down into plastic collars.
Like those three gray elephants
you saw one day in late November
through a blur of snow,
standing in a stripped cornfield
outside Indianapolis,
left behind
when the failing circus sneaked away.

SLEEPING BEAUTY IV

Like I told Lurette, "What's all the fuss?
It isn't as if we don't have the same old house.
Last summer we biked cross-country,
Mom and I. The others went to Granny's. It took
all summer. We biked Oregon to Denver.
Back roads all way east. Camped out. It was
something Mom wanted to do. Here's Mom, forty-five!
The divorce goes through. Mom gets custody of all eight
of us. So what's the fuss? Dad's this charismatic
math professor. He can't help it. I love my dad.
So what? We backpacked. Mom lost thirty pounds. I
lived on trail mix. It makes me sick to think of nuts.
Mom was crazy. She had this map. I mean she wouldn't
ask. We'd get lost. Bears? Rattlers? Just the two
of us in a nylon tent. 'No sweat,' Mom kept saying,
'no sweat.' She wouldn't relax. Wanted
to put more miles on. Hazel's really sweet. You know
her florist shop? It's not her fault that she and Dad . . .
Mom's always been so dumb. I mean she doesn't even watch
TV. Always doing laundry, P.T.A. I think everyone knew but
Mom what was going on. Not me! I'm not like my mom. We
never really got along. Does my mom read? She's a martyr.
Martyrs don't read. I read Danielle Steel books, and hey!
I read Stephen King, too. Mom has not taken care of her teeth.
She's still got them but they overlap. I wore braces. I
suffered for my teeth. I'm like my dad. He lets me babysit
the new kid. It makes Mom so mad she gets pains in her chest.
Now Mom's into karate. I'm so embarrassed."

THE MOTHERS

Working out of mind, the wind says,
I take little or nothing.
I exchange one thing for another.
I rearrange.

Bother, the sand says,
she will not let me be,
slap, slap.

I cannot help it.
I have no bones of my own.
I am the mother of everything.
I am the lap of the world.
Dissolve in me, says the ocean.

We are the white eyes, sing the Himalayas.
We are the frozen cones of eternity.
We are the paradise of goats and tigers.
We hide the Abominable.
Only the wind,
only the melting snows
can wear us away grain by grain.
We are the land of the impossible.
We are the mothers of sand.

The sun flings her fiery hair
on the dark body of the universe.
Here are my offspring, she croons.
I will eat them all in time;
I will grow at one with my dark love —

the nothingness of nothing undefiled.
But they follow me like ducklings,
my piteous maimed little ones
with their cracked moons;
and my close, once perfect,
blue suffering child, ravaged.
I am the mother of sorrow.

THE SAD VOICE OF THE HUBBLE

As I am the eyes of your eyes,
searching for black holes,
darkness that is and is not,
iris of swallowed light;

so beneath me the mortal wounds,
the malaise of the parent body;
its sensual skin of sadness.

The radiation that touches the body,
the body of this illusion,
is the random of photons, singing.

With your wrinkled palms,
with your stiff extended fingers,
you rose and floated around me;
strange bulky angels.

As I am borne out here
on the violence of consuming,
the violence of starvation;

I am here like the suave mortician,
to help you pick out the casket.

THE UNPLANTED

Little water mother,
we see you from our empty sockets,
as we orbit misfired from Vladivostok,
the two of us married forever, Sergei and I.
We watched our blue watered, white clotted pearl
fall away from us into its jeweled clutch of gravity.
Circling beyond hope we enter and leave,
enter and leave, freeze dried in our capsule,
two seeds in a pod.

THE JOURNEY

Hearing phrases like . . . the Great Rift Valley,
one mountain in the brain
sends signals to the other.
Under the bloody bone,
that little world
where everything is so significant;
the valley where the mothers
and fathers slogged
and tore flesh;
the world's cranium,
so delicate and scarred.

Phrases like . . . the Marianas Trench,
deep miasmas, miles of silt;
equinox after equinox,
when everything that drifted down
begins to rise;
the edge of one abyss
upon another;
sheer escarpments,
and the climb, the long climb
against the impossible.

IN THE FAST LANE

Three men just sprinted
through the turgid crowd,
hot to catch a train
already pulled away on
Track Five. Here they are
underground — each in a
modish suit, soul-searching
tie, computerized watch,
every breath scheduled.
Who can deny their shared
psychosis? Of course
they're tired. Not physically
tired as that flyspeck
window washer
strapped up near the jet stream
who overreached
his squeegee. No. It's
a vein-letting metal exhaustion —
messages of chips, shredded
memos covertly hidden in
inner pockets; and all this
medical trash washed up
on the public beaches.

Sun on snow, panes of light
peel against the walls.
A red supermarket geranium on the windowsill.
In the cupboard there is a persimmon.

Water boils in a yellow pan.
The dog eats, hunching away the cat.
I swallow my vitamin.

Twenty years ago on a hill above the Pacific,
I learned to add one ice cube to a cup of instant coffee.
My friends, sleeping in drills of other gardens,
lay in their shaded rooms behind the terrace
where I watched for migrating whales
to surface from their deep corridors.

This persimmon is tropical, soft and ripe,
large as a pear,
not like those nuggets that fell in our schoolyard
here in the Midwest.
Unless we waited until they were freckled with frost,
one bite would pucker our mouths and shrivel our lips.

Light moves slanting down along the plaster.
Back under the flowered comfort my feet are not warm.
The cat sags over the edge of the bed.
Gradually chewing its works, the electric clock grinds faster
and faster. I eat this plump persimmon with a spoon.

The ritual rhyming music of the humpback whales,
their resonant booming
wanders through me as through a great hall
echoing violins, tubas, drums.
I see microphones plumb-lined down among them
as they move in protocol
in their leviathan delayed timing.

ANOTHER REPORT

Under the snowberry bushes
when the snow rots;
crystal ruin.
These are the ice palaces
of the snow fleas.
You hear a slight sizzling;
pop, pop. That black smudge
on the surface of snow
is the resident army on
bivouac; exercised generals
leaping for the opposite sex.
Or are they? Maybe it's
the other way around.
They are all leaping
more or less.
It looks like they're
leaping for sex, but
as to who is leaping for whom
and what's its gender,
is difficult to detect.
Specks tend to blur.
A rough graph needs to be
spread with enough spread
so you can make checks
against your usual range of
normal, rough, deviant, kinky,
incestuous, peculiar,
abnormal, definitely
strange and your

really really weird
way out stuff. Right now,
here in the field, as it were,
what's going on down there
is anybody's guess.

GOOD FRIDAY ON THE BUS

Conversations behind you;
each wanting to get a lifetime
squeezed between Cleveland and Erie.
They drag it out,
the ordinary day to day;
sitting beside one another
without listening:
their families, their operations,
the virtues of the Pentecostal.
But the child
sitting next to you is silent.
After many miles
he is inspired to tell you
he has made an egg for his sister
but he has varnished it so
she can't crack it open.
He smiles.
Fields of stubble;
hay in vague shapes like kneeling animals.
Marbleized as a lake of ice, clouds,
separating pieces of puzzle drifting away.
Looking up into reflecting blue,
the camouflage of stars,
you think, as you must,
that what you see is the way it is,
the way it will always be.

THE REAL SOUTHWEST BY GREYHOUND

At an undesignated point in the desert,
the Immigration Service's truck waits for the bus.
Meanwhile, on the Greyhound, the passengers
from Ohio are reading their Bibles.
Outside the bus it is dry, useless; one or two scrounging cattle.
If they look out the windows, the passengers
from Ohio keep their fingers in their Bibles.
They probably think — outside there, how real is real?
How much of that is made up?
But not the Mexicans. They are talking in soft rills.
They have rolls of blankets and cooking pots
stuffed into paper shopping bags up on the rack.
They are worried about the immigration officer.
Even if you have your own face on a card,
it can be tough in that long moment of silence
before he hands it back.

DECEMBER USA

Cryptic
cracks
between clouds,
like ice
breaking
up in March
when the
fishing huts
lurch
and begin
to sink.
But that's
looking forward.
The first
heavy snow
is on its way;
gray cortex,
stripped down
saplings;
skin of crystals.
The deep
sometimes
death
sleep of
toads;
cloth of
those who
will rise,
hidden
under logs,

in crevices.
With bruised tissue,
fingers without
flesh;
the leper
of gifts
outside
the gates,
December's
albino face
comes toward us
crying alms
for the unclean,
the homeless,
the untouchables.

FOR MY DEAD RED-HAIRED MOTHER

I loved a red-haired girl.
Freud knew it was a wicked thing to do.
This is how all poems begin.
Sometime after the age of two
I beat the Adam in me black and blue.
Infant, wicked infant!
I threw my love outside
and grew into a bride.

You and I reflecting in our bones
the sea and sky,
we dressed ourselves as flesh,
we learned to lie.

Dearly beloved,
forgive me for that mean and meager self,
that now would mingle
but must first die.

SIMPLICITY

I must retrace my exact steps on the crust,
or I will sink knee-deep in snow.
Kneeling to dip water from the open center of the brook —
between the ridged armies of black trees,
a splinter of light along the line of frost.
Clear as a printed map,
wrinkled skin on a cup of boiled milk —
the mountains of the moon, a full disc edging up.
Dreading all day to come here for this necessary water,
temperature dropping toward zero;
under the ice the water's muscular flow,
its insane syllables, is like a human voice.
Inside the house, sleep, sleep.
I brace myself to lift the weight on either hand.
Picking up my full kettle and bucket
and fitting my feet inside their frozen tracks,
I return under the risen moon,
following my shadow.

LULLABY

New Wave babies
kiss their computers.
Good night Orno and Porno.
They put on their Hug-Me-Tites.
Pucker and poo.
Program the buttons.
Karoom! Kaboom!
$E=mc^2$
So long. Toodle-oo.

THE MOTHER'S EYES

All morning when talking to their mother,
the grievance is the other sister;
the oldest, the middle or the youngest.
Between them their bored fingers scratch
the frost paintings on the window glass.
They rip the delicate
filigreed mountain passes, the streams
in the deep gorges. They crush the exquisite
crystals with their fingernails.
Sunlight filters through their scratches.
The mother leans down and puts her eyes to the window
and sees the transfigured world outside.
The snow has stopped burying the house, the road,
the small orchard. And in a miracle, even their voices,
the frail knives of their words on the bitter air,
cut little holes that the mother can see through.

THE ARTIST

Either he put himself in the painting
after he arrived or before he started;
before he went down to that place from
which he is returning. In the painting
he is facing along the upward slope, his back
bent, leaning forward. You see his
wrapped legs and feet, his heavy pack.
He is halfway up on the disappearing
path; a small figure. The scroll
is four hundred years old.
There is no one else in the painting.
The brushwork is delicate. If you
look down, the footbridge he crossed is
a quarter mile below. Below that, the river
is a thread in the ravine. These details
are in the lower half of the painting.
He has been traveling all day. You see
that he can't make it before dark. The
temple appears to be about a mile
farther horizontally along the slope.
It thrusts out of bare rock,
well above the tree line; a shadow on the
sky. You see now that there is a curtain
of snow blowing. You see he can't make it.
And yet there is no way to stop him. He is
still going up and he is still only half way.

FROM THE WINDOW

There go spring freshets wearing down rocks
under a hill on the highway to Louisville,
and a flock of white chickens
putting a trashy yard to shame
with their sleek pullet feathers.
All of last year's oak leaves are on the ground.
Yearlings browse on the slopes.
The bus jounces up and down on frost heaves.
Ropes of little birds taggle across
a flat gray cumulus, and a man on a tractor
has just turned over an entire field of red clay.

COLUMBUS, OHIO

Practicing some silent underwater drift,
molded in plastic primary blue and yellow
bus station seats; like paper cutouts,
scissored replicas snipped from folded newspapers
to entertain a child,
these homeless bodies of men.
Hunched in layers, ten of them
asleep in hard cup chairs;
their feet in rotting shoes,
the time, three A.M.,
when suddenly one of them
stands up and stretches
and walks away yawning;
as if this is a decent home in the suburbs,
with children, arms and legs spread out
like baby starfish in their acrylic blankets.
As if he is leaving the soft mound of his wife's
secret body,
and going into their kitchen
to fill his thermos with hot coffee.
As if nothing is impossible,
as if it is an ordinary day.

MUSIC

Even here on the upthrust rocks
and algae-blooming rivers,
rhythms of light. Here, where you find
yourself among inheritors of the indentured,
with highways criss-crossed like shoelaces,
streets named for Schubert and Beethoven;
and on the G.E. plant and shells of shoe factories,
the same sun, white as on a plaster wall in Athens.
This very moment, here, a skimpy evergreen
whistles with a bluff rush of air
and the updraft catches birds, even stout pigeons
dipping for snow fleas. And these disregarded scavengers,
the city's unconscious grace, rise in a flock;
their shadows like musical notations
erased across the parking lot.

AFTER WINTER

Thunder is subliminal. Even rain,
fluttering the air inside this room.
It is so old, continents
have broken up and come again.

You think it is traffic shaking the house.
You have forgotten thunder,
that rumbly rush and breaker of glaze.
The earth under you trembles,
its great self coming out of the cave,
the yellowed snow where the piss melts.

But your pulse beats with a flood within.
Your body naked, seized with its own grief;
turning over everything,
beginning without end, muttering.

THE OTHERS

It is autumn. The indoor fig tree
desires to do as the others,
to shed its hysterical fingers.
It sees wasps in sunlight
making continuous love with the woodbin,
possessing it, chewing little bits of it,
making a thin paper
on which to send passionate messages.

The fig tree feels like a child.
It would like to trade its leaves
for something hectic, palladium.
Outside in the steady rain, maples
continue to strip carotene, xanthophyll,
transparent leaf cells
stretched like gauze over burned hands.

LOOKING FOR SIGNS

Charles and I turn right at the privet hedge.
We are six brisk feet stopping at random stations.
Alone on a porch, a baby behind bars
waves in a private language.
We have just moved in, 2nd floor, number 22.
We cross at the corner. No traffic except for birds.
This is an old established neighborhood.
Each lawn is mowed. Each driveway fresh asphalt.
It is Sunday; quiet as the color of washed blue.
Charles poops. We are embarrassed and walk on.

Street after street of silent well-kept houses,
embalmed with beds of marigolds, more explicit than words;
gratuitous designs of manicured slopes;
but, yes, a sweet disorderly fall of yellow leaves.
Thereupon, to the bells of nearby St. Blessed Ascension,
we pause at one aberrant yard with broken palings,
a house of uncurtained windows painted jonquil yellow,
to see from this angle the unlikely bodies
of three middle-aged cars jacked up on cement blocks
under the maples at the back,
where the uncut lawn is blessed with flowering weeds;
and although there is no one visible,
we are made strangely happy and walk on.

THE CORD

Here is the body
like a forlorn child,
sitting on a park bench,
it scarcely knows where you are.
Who can blame it for dreaming up
impossible places to scratch?
Sometimes when it has you alone in a bed
it waits for that concentration
of meaningless pleasure,
the sad imprisoned feet
that work so hard
rubbing their soles in the sheets,
while the body pulls you in
on the long drift cord
from the edge of the universe.
"Here," it says, "touch me here."

THAT MOMENT

The mineral vapor rising from the sidewalks
on the shaded side where we met in the morning,
let loose from our acceptable ways
into a forbidden rendezvous.
Midwest, mid-30's, USA;
the coffee shop beside a garage in Urbana, Illinois.
In the warm sleepwalking odor of a nearby bakery,
delicate mold from damp bricks, the deep murmur
of the prairie coming into us
like mica, like radiation, silently
tearing apart our fibers, altering our ganglia.
Under the marquee of the gas station,
a slapdash coffee stopover,
two tables in a lean-to beside the garage,
five cents a cup with buttered toast.
I remember every pore of your scarred face,
every gesture of your long fingers.
Those gifts so unexplored, passionate
thud of the portable Underwood,
fast as the fastest typist in the world;
those surreal novels now lying in a drawer,
lost to everyone but me.
I live in the mounting paper of loss.
Speaking to you, as we sat there
in the terror of our own violence,
even the odor of gasoline, provocative, sexual;
the glaze of this skew in time, twisting us
as at that moment the twisted iris
on the long translucent stalks were trembling
open, the folded tissues of themselves,
their opalescent throats, opening
to the unfolding of the miracle.

FINDING MYSELF

Thursday, the 20th of July,
came to me and said,
I will give you this one elastic day.
Snap it shut or stretch it like bread dough.
So I put my hands in kneading and pulling.
It was a gauze-bag day.
The blue bell flower opened at the tip of its stalk.
I am a body not equipped to take every flag down hill,
but looking at all the exits and entrances,
I chose white wine in a plain glass goblet,
and wearing a flannel nightgown,
I went barefoot into the uncut grass.
The temperature rose.
The yeast began to work.
Every spider took to the air.
The cells of my skin puffed and tugged
and with a great shout let go their tethers
until looking up I saw myself like a cloud,
like ectoplasm, like an angel
among the branches of trees.
Then peeling layer after layer
I went to it letting go,
until only the elemental worm remained
letting itself down
on a string of spittle.

COFFEE AND SWEET ROLLS

When I remember the dingy hotels
where we lay reading Baudelaire,
your long elegant fingers, the nervous ritual
of your cigarette; you, a young poet working
in the steel mills; me, married
to a dull chemical engineer.
Fever of having nothing to lose;
no luggage, a few books, the streetcar.
In the manic shadow of Hitler, the guttural
monotony of war; often just enough money
for the night. Rising together in the clanking
elevators to those rooms where we lay like embryos;
helpless in the desire to be completed;
to be issued out into the terrible world.

All night, sighing and waking, insatiable.
At daylight, counting our change, you would go for coffee.
Then, lying alone, I heard the sirens,
the common death of everything and again
the little girl I didn't know
all in white in a white casket;
the boy I once knew, smashed with his motorcycle
into the pavement, and what was said,
"made a wax figure for his funeral,"
came into me. I had never touched the dead.
Always the lock unclicked and you were back,
our breakfast in a paper sack.
What I waited for was the tremor in your voice.
In those rooms with my eyes half open,
I memorized for that austere and silent woman
who waited in the future,

who for years survived on this fiction;
so even now I can see you standing thin and naked,
the shy flush of your rising cock pointed toward heaven,
as you pull down the dark window shade.

THE SOLUTION

My friend the Supermarket
talks to me through my friend the Television Set.
They tell me I am not lonely.
"Come to me," Super says.
"Have an electric clock and a big cucumber.
Very cheap.
You can set yourself to go off with the alarm."
They take me in my sleep to the shopping plaza
and show me temptations in plastic.
"All this can be yours," they say,
"gorge yourself."

SCHEHERAZADE IS MAILED
AND NAILED IN FIVE DAYS

At ten to seven on November 24th, 1990,
Scheherazade is translated into the new world,
a little out of synch,
and still telling the story of Sinbad.
However, she arrives from Baghdad,
where an American soldier unrolled her
out of a cave in a hillside,
thinking she was a small dormant thing.
He was looking for shade, a little privacy,
in the act of writing a letter to his mother.
Scheherazade crept into the envelope
and here she is, reconstituted.
Well, they went for "I Dream of Jeannie," so
who knows?
Yes, now she is afloat on the Alleghenies
in a second-floor flat with a genie mongrel,
still telling her stories
in order to save her head.
She looks into the animal's sad eyes.
It is just after a day of feasting.
The feast is done, the cheese rolls lie warmed over.
Alas, her kalif has been gone for hundreds of years.
Scheherazade has forgotten the executioner.
But she is still walking barefoot over the spikes of words.
How many veils drawn aside
to look into the pit of the kalif's heart?
His high-bridged nose, nostrils disdainful.
She thinks, will he never fall asleep?
But Scheherazade is, after all,
in love with her own voice.

She looks around this miraculous dwelling —
the cheap chest of drawers,
her now useless intimate apparel,
and the finally impotent rug.
She hears the dead kalif sigh.
Scheherazade has no choice.
In this place my lord, she begins to fabricate,
sin is not so bad; in fact, it's the best
to be had. But it is overcast,
and my listeners are understandably bored.
She is referring to the dog.
What can I tell you about this old lamp,
you whose eyes have sucked into their skull?
She both knows and does not know that the kalif
is dead, that she is a figment herself in a story,
that the story is dying too and the storyteller.
Still, let me unclasp this brooch and touch the instrument.
It is the dance of a mouse, running across the sand
or the memory of yourself,
descending and ascending the marble stair,
leaning from the arched windows
to be other than you are,
to be elsewhere.
She is sitting on the rug.
The rug is kaput.
She's stuck.

November 25th: Scheherazade is cheating at solitaire.
Now her stories are hewn out of newscasts.
The kalif is always looking the other way.
The dog sleeps, hooding his eyes of fire,
his demon's disguise.
Where is that sorcerer in torn clothes,
his cracked voice whining under the windows:

new lamps for old?
Instead, it snows.
Then the clouds are snatched away by whips
coming between the mountains.
Then the blue blind eye of nothing squints down.
She yawns, and lays out the cards.
Scheherazade and the dog are unaccountably fat.
The flying rug still does not raise them above the floor.
They sleep and wake only to eat or stand at the window,
to be amused by the chain of lights on the hills,
the moving cars, the infinite black veil.
Overhead the kalif's descendants fly
from continent to continent
with the smoothness of oil.
Now they control the world.
The former stories of Scheherazade
are small baggage for an old camel.

November 26th: she continues chatting to the air,
inventing out of the new atmosphere:
to be the other on the Aleutian tundra,
to be a strong man dying on a golf course,
to be a drummer whose heart stops on the stage,
to be a middle-aged woman smoking her way through cancer,
to be a lover, loving in murderous rage.
And here she digresses.
The tundra, if it is bare, is a ghost place
where the sky falls into itself,
where the Arctic birds run into the wind to rise,
their feathers like fractals,
their nests hidden in the wildflowers.
And Scheherazade dances on bare feet.
She closes her eyes.
She forgets her other lives

like the one where the painted mime
wearing a g-string and pasties,
a coarse blond wig over his Egyptian hair
drives at midnight to pick her up
at the door of the theater.
She murmurs, my kalif, as always, I hear
in the canyons and caves
the sighing of the poor.
And here in this place, the sirens,
the flashing lights
and the magic box,
the picture, always brilliant with blood
and always the echo of laughter.
To escape for a moment, she sings of the lover.
He is a dancer, he comes from the Mongol hordes
over the steppes, over the onyx ice.
His mother, a weaver of rugs,
rubs his skin with oil of roses.
He wears an embroidered vest,
silk leggings.
He leaps, he clicks his heels,
he clashes the scimitar.
His eyes are slant,
his cheeks cleaved to the bone;
his laugh is harsh. She listens —
Nothing.
He is gone a thousand moons
into the mountains of the forgotten.

He could be this man, living in a doorway,
or this man crossing the backyards
collecting bottles,
or this man, with a Saturday night special
in his hip pocket.

Forgive me, she sings, for loving this man in fear,
for my body that sleeps in an aggregate of deaths.
One story out of another,
so many inside one skin
like the spider's egg,
a world inside the self,
wrinkled, swelling, a heated balloon rising;
the voices, the costumes.
I am a multitude, sings the head.
Why have I only one body?

Time is falling inward,
an imploding sphere.
Scheherazade drones on. By now it is November 28th.
She snaps the switch
and lets the sorcerer's box speak for her.
These stories, my kalif, she hastens to say,
are repetitious,
the same old formula.
You will see, of course, misogyny, sadism,
violence, thieves in the streets, rape,
death of the spirit, blood, blood brothers.
It is all here.
She speaks of the merchandise,
bandits dancing with swords of fire, and then
war and the spoils of war. And afterward,
the trials, my kalif,
the usual trials, as yours,
always the hands cut off
and so forth. After a while,
again she is bored.
She grows deaf to the mechanical laughter.
Her multidimensional vision sees for miles,
multitudes frozen, the sorcerer's poison

pumping into their veins. They are all fat,
as the fattest mogul. In front of their boxes
they fall asleep and snore.
But she tries to speak again.
A few grow very rich,
as you, my kalif; the rest become slaves.
Some lie down on the flat fitted rocks. Children
shiver in cast-out wrappings. It is all the same.
The women are tangled in the usual purdah,
as under you, my lord, the same ritual,
although there are small differences. Here each kalif's
kalif has a replacement, an inheritor, cunningly made
and hollow, where the magician hides.
Still she is bored. She begins to sigh
and she cannot dance. She feels no fugitive joy.
Once her stories were endless; now a gray wrack
of rags, she lies down, drunk; an habitual weeper.
The dead kalif cannot be charmed.
The flesh falls away under his splitting shroud.
The dog snores. At last Scheherazade comes face
to face with the executioner.
He comes through a thousand thousand doors.
They slam like the doors to the showers at Auschwitz.
You poets and lovers!
He faxes her a smile.
It was only a matter of time, he says.
You were always ours.

ONCE MORE

O my crows,
when you return in April,
your harsh voices,
your dark selves
rowing the raw air,
you males who made it home
to the mountain;
this shadow below you
in the orchard
is me,
triumphant,
listening
to rocks smash downstream
in the snowmelt.

ABOUT THE AUTHOR

Ruth Stone was born in 1915 in Roanoke, Virginia.
Her numerous honors include the Bunting Fellowship, two
Guggenheim Fellowships, the Delmore Schwartz Award, and the
Shelley Memorial Award. She is Professor of English at the State
University of New York, Binghamton. She lives in Vermont.

COLOPHON

The text of this book is composed in Palatino.
Photograph of Ruth Stone by Jan Freeman.
Cover design by Mary Mendell.
Drawing on cover by Siena Sanderson, b. 1956, untitled pastel
on paper, 30" x 22", 1992. Siena Sanderson lives in New Mexico.